BURY ST EDM

and Beyond

'The nicest town in the world'
William Cobbett, essayist and traveller

THE EDMUND STORY

Bury St Edmunds, literally 'the place of St Edmund' in Saxon English, grew up around one of the most powerful monasteries in medieval England. Originally a small settlement known as Beodricksworth, it was chosen by the Saxon king Sigebert as the setting for a modest monastic community in the 7th century.

It was the enshrinement here nearly three centuries later of the martyred King Edmund that was to bring fame and fortune to the town. Ruler of East Anglia and a devout Christian, Edmund was captured by raiding Vikings in AD 869. Legend has it that on refusing to renounce his faith the king was tied to a tree and shot full of arrows. His head was then unceremoniously cut off and thrown into a wood. When his followers searched for it, they heard a voice crying, 'Here, here, here!'. Following the cries they found the severed head guarded by a wolf. When laid in the coffin, Edmund's head and body were mysteriously united leaving only a faint red mark – the sign of a true saint. Many miracles were subsequently attributed to the power of Edmund, and he was patron saint of England until the dragon-slaying George was awarded the title in more militant times.

It was King Cnut (or Canute; c.994–1035) who established a Benedictine community at Bury St Edmunds in the early 11th century.

◄ *An embroidery (1982) from the cathedral, by Sybil Andrews, depicting scenes from the life of St Edmund.*

▲ *Living history at West Stow Anglo-Saxon Village.*

◀ *St Edmund: a statue by Elisabeth Frink near the west front of the ruined abbey.*

The legacy of the abbots pervades the town. King Cnut, meanwhile, is commemorated on a shopfront in Cornhill in his best remembered pose – getting his feet wet on the seashore.

At West Stow, just north-west of Bury St Edmunds, an Anglo-Saxon village has been reconstructed on the site of a former settlement using the tools and techniques of Edmund's era. Home to wild boar, chickens and – at certain times of the year – Saxon villagers, it tells the story of everyday life in Anglo-Saxon times.

Edmund's story continues into the new millennium. In the precinct of the former abbey, now in ruins, stand two beautiful churches. One, St Edmundsbury Cathedral, was first built by Abbot Anselm in the 12th century. The later 16th-century rebuilding is attributed to John Wastell, who completed King's College Chapel, Cambridge. For many years it has remained the last incomplete cathedral in Britain, but now a 140-feet (43-metre) Gothic-style tower is being built to celebrate 1,000 years of the St Edmund story – and to be a beacon of faith for many more centuries to come.

BURY FIRSTS

Baldwin (Abbot 1065–97) was one of the very first town planners. As well as being the personal physician of two kings, he laid out the town of Bury St Edmunds.

3

GATEWAYS TO THE GREAT ABBEY

'The sun does not shine . . . on an abbey more famous, whether we regard its endowments, its size or its magnificence. You would aver that the abbey was a town in itself.'

John Leland

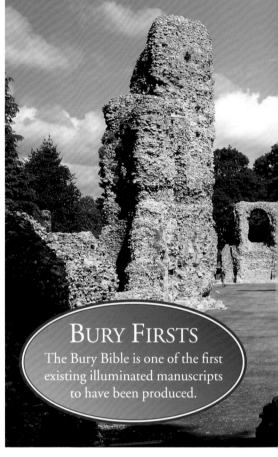

In medieval times the Abbey of St Edmund drew pilgrims from across Europe. Entering through the Norman Tower at the foot of Churchgate Street, they would pass through the bronze doors of the west front into the splendidly painted abbey church where the saint's shrine stood.

The tower, built between 1120 and 1148, is the most complete surviving building of the original abbey complex. It now houses the bells of the neighbouring cathedral. Behind it, the west front has been converted into private residences. At one end is the visitor centre which tells the story of Edmund and the abbey, assisted by a scale model outside. The centre is inside Samson's

BURY FIRSTS
The Bury Bible is one of the first existing illuminated manuscripts to have been produced.

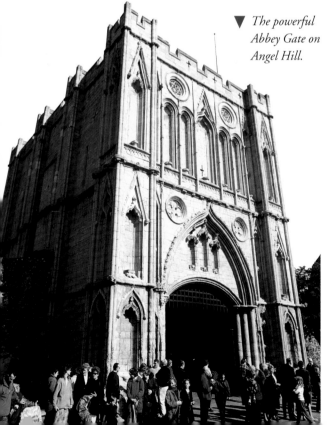

▼ *The powerful Abbey Gate on Angel Hill.*

Tower, named after a famous abbot whose grave can still be found among the abbey ruins, and who was immortalized in the chronicles of Brother Jocelin of Brakelond, the abbey's best-known historian.

The monks of Bury St Edmunds also dealt with a wide range of secular matters. Parliament was held at the abbey, and kings and courtiers often visited. Merchants and tradespeople did business with the monks, and local people came to air grievances and seek medical advice. There was a separate gateway for such affairs, today called the Abbey Gate. This proved a focal point for the frustrations of the townspeople in medieval times and was torn down in 1327 during an uprising by a crowd of 3,000. During the riot, the abbot was abducted and several

monks killed. Twenty years later, the gate was rebuilt on the present site, this time with arrow slits, a guards' room, a portcullis and a great door to keep out troublesome visitors.

In the 16th century the abbey was taken apart on the orders of Henry VIII, during the Dissolution of the Monasteries. Little is left to indicate the abbey's scale and grandeur. The largest of the surviving stone columns is thought to be about one third of its former height. Enter through the Abbey Gate today, however, and you are greeted by the stunning public gardens that now cover the Great Court and surround the intriguing ruins. Prize-winning flower beds, lawns, an aviary and a host of other attractions together form the much-loved Abbey Gardens which are the pride of Bury St Edmunds.

▲ *An artist's impression of the abbey by W. Kimber Hardie.*

▲ *The dramatic ruins of what was, in medieval times, one of the wealthiest abbeys in Britain.*

◀ *The Norman Tower, built by Abbot Anselm, forms a striking gateway to the abbey precinct.*

5

THE MAGNA CARTA LEGEND

At Runnymede, at Runnymede,
Your rights were won at Runnymede!
No freeman shall be fined or bound,
Or dispossessed of freehold ground,
Except by lawful judgment found
And passed upon him by his peers.
Forget not, after all these years,
The Charter signed at Runnymede.

Rudyard Kipling

The early years of the 13th century were a turbulent time for England. The country was ruled by King John, the cruel and greedy king immortalized in the tales of Robin Hood.

Wars were a constant feature of medieval life and John was in continual need of funds from the barons to prop up his ailing foreign campaigns. As he became more desperate, his feudal claims grew ever more exorbitant and the brutality with which he enforced them knew no bounds.

Defeat for John in France in July 1214 brought the barons to breaking point. It is said that on St Edmund's Day in November that year, 25 of them gathered at the high altar of the Abbey of St Edmund to meet with the Archbishop of Canterbury. Resolved to curtail the king's demands and brutal behaviour, they decided to force him to sign a charter of liberties. King John acceded to their demands almost a year later at Runnymede, near Windsor, and Magna Carta, the 'Great Charter', came into being. Over the centuries it has become the foundation of all constitutional government.

▶ *One of the original copies of Magna Carta (1215), and an artist's impression of its seal.*

6

While there has been debate over the historical accuracy of the Bury St Edmunds meeting, it is nevertheless enshrined in the town's motto. Summing up Magna Carta and St Edmund in one breath, this runs *Sacrarium Regis, Cunabula Legis* – Shrine of the King, Cradle of the Law.

Among the barons responsible for Magna Carta were Richard de Clare, Earl of Gloucester, and his son Gilbert de Clare. You can find the ruined former seat of this local family in the Castle Country Park, Clare, to the south of Bury St Edmunds. The shields of the Magna Carta barons can be spotted around St Edmundsbury Cathedral.

▲ *The Ancient House Museum at Clare, the village where two of the Magna Carta barons lived.*

◀ *A plaque at the site of the abbey high altar.*

NEAR THIS SPOT
ON THE 20ᵀᴴ NOVEMBER A.D. 1214.
CARDINAL LANGTON & THE BARONS
SWORE AT Sᵀ EDMUND'S ALTAR
THAT THEY WOULD OBTAIN FROM
KING JOHN
THE RATIFICATION OF
MAGNA CHARTA.

SACRARIUM REGIS·CUNABULA LEGIS

▲ *The crest and motto of Bury St Edmunds, immortalizing the legend of Magna Carta.*

◀ *The barons and archbishop meet at the high altar of the Abbey of St Edmund: a Victorian artist's impression.*

THE HERVEY HERITAGE

Three miles south of Bury St Edmunds stands one of the most unusual stately homes in England. Ickworth House is a rotunda with two wings, owned for many centuries by the Hervey family, the Earls (later Marquesses) of Bristol, and now cared for by The National Trust. Built in 1795 and later remodelled by the Hervey heirs, it is set in many acres of historic gardens and parkland landscaped by 'Capability' Brown. Its breathtaking, chandelier-hung rooms and collections of fine art make it a true treasure house. But this didn't, it seems, stop the younger Herveys from roller skating down the lengthy corridors.

One resident of Ickworth, Elizabeth Hervey, the second wife of the 1st Earl of Bristol, set her heart upon a fashionable town house in Bury St Edmunds. Today known as Manor House Museum, the new residence was built in 1738. With its diminutive ballroom and modest dining room, Manor House provides a striking contrast to the Ickworth House we know today. Here Elizabeth was able to indulge her taste for social gatherings – and gambling. Sadly, the poor lady died within three years of

▲ *History comes to life at Manor House Museum.*

▶ *The Pompeian room, one of many delights on view to the public at Ickworth House.*

BURY FIRSTS

Frederick William John Augustus Hervey, 7th Marquess of Bristol (1954 – 99), became the first peer of the realm to be expelled from Australia, for failing to disclose his drug convictions.

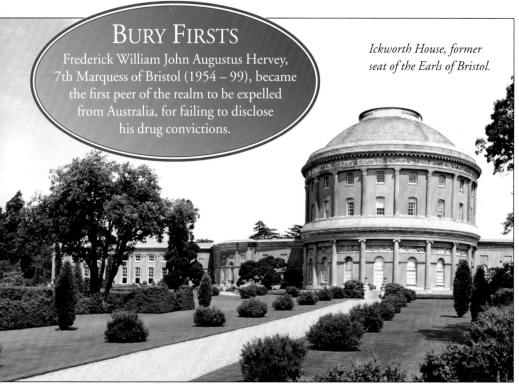

Ickworth House, former seat of the Earls of Bristol.

the completion of her town house. It is now a museum of costume, horology and fine arts and a magical place to visit, especially at the moment when 500 clocks and watches strike the hour simultaneously.

The Abbey Gardens were formerly owned by the Marquess of Bristol, and it was he who had them laid out in 1831 by Nathaniel Hodson as a botanical garden. For some time they remained subscription gardens but were opened as a public park in 1911 to mark the coronation of George V. Some of Hodson's original specimens remain, and the gardens today are known for their horticultural innovation. They are one of only three places in England where you can see the Princess Marie-José dahlia.

▼ *One of the exquisite timepieces on display at Manor House Museum.*

9

BURY AT WAR

Suffolk's gentle landscape and proximity to mainland Europe made it a perfect location for air bases during the Second World War. During that time, many bomber groups of the American air force were stationed here, and memorials in local villages commemorate the men who flew from nearby airfields. Two miles (4km) east of Bury St Edmunds, the old control tower at Rougham marks the wartime home of the 94th Bomber Group. It is currently being restored as a museum which tells of the tower's role in the Second World War.

John Appleby, an American airforceman, wrote an account of the time he spent touring the beautiful churches and countryside while stationed here. Called *Suffolk Summer*, it is sold locally, the proceeds going towards the upkeep of the Appleby Rose Garden in the Abbey Gardens. The rose garden also contains a memorial stone and a bench made from a bomber – not to be sat upon too quickly on hot summer days. These days one of Europe's biggest bomber fleets is stationed at RAF Lakenheath

▲ *An American crew prepare their plane for another flight over Germany.*

BURY FIRSTS

The first bombing raids on Germany in the Second World War took place from local air bases Wattisham and Mildenhall in December 1940.

▼ *During the Second World War many thousands of Americans were stationed at airfields in the Bury St Edmunds area.*

to the north-west of Bury
St Edmunds, the setting for the
James Bond movie *Tomorrow
Never Dies*. RAF Mildenhall, close
by, organizes an impressive air fête
each spring that attracts around
300,000 people.

*The seat in the
Appleby Rose Garden
which was made from
an American B52
'Flying Fortress'
bomber.*

Bury St Edmunds also has
strong connections with the Army
and is especially proud of its long
relationship with the Suffolk Regiment. This was first raised by the
Duke of Norfolk in 1685 at the
command of James II to assist against the threatened
Monmouth Rebellion. In 1873, its depot was established in Bury St Edmunds and in 1878 barracks were
built which still make an imposing sight on Out
Risbygate. The museum of local history, Moyse's Hall,
has a gallery dedicated to the regimental collection.

*The badge of the
Suffolk Regiment.*

St Mary's Church on Crown Street contains the
Suffolk Regiment Chapel and the Birkenhead Mem-
orial commemorating soldiers who drowned off the
South African coast in February 1852. The expression
'Women and children first' is said to have originated
from the bravery of the regiment's men in that disaster.

St Mary's is the civic church and houses
the Mayor's seat. Its hammerbeam roof
with carved angels spans the longest
parish church aisle in England.
Here too is the tomb of Mary
Tudor (1496–1533), sister
of Henry VIII, queen
consort of Louis XII and
Duchess of Suffolk.

*The Appleby Rose Garden with, beyond, the
east end of St Edmundsbury Cathedral.*

FARMING COUNTRY

Stand at the top of Abbeygate Street and you can glimpse the fields that surround Bury St Edmunds. Changing from wintry brown to all shades of green, yellow and blue as the year marches on, they are a constant reminder of the town's place in the farming community. At harvest time, trucks go to and fro with their cargoes of turnip and sugar beet (Bury St Edmunds has Britain's largest sugar beet processing plant) and the cathedral is always packed for the county's Harvest Festival when displays of farm animals and machinery appear on Angel Hill.

Traditional villages preserve their windmills and watermills in tribute to an era gone by, and Rede Hall Farm Park, 6 miles (10km) south of the town, still farms using techniques from the 1950s. Rede Hall is one of the few places where visitors can meet the 'Suffolk Trinity', a trio of farm animals composed of the Suffolk Punch heavy horse, the Red Poll cow and the Suffolk sheep.

Much of the land around Bury St Edmunds is covered with vineyards, notably those yielding the prize-winning grapes of Wyken Hall in Stanton to the north-east. The traditions of brewing and wine-

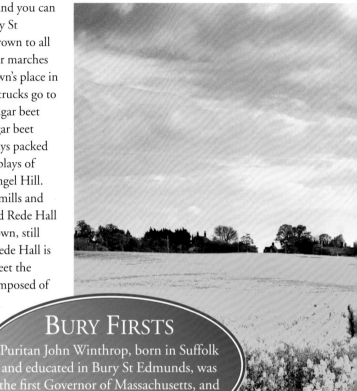

BURY FIRSTS

Puritan John Winthrop, born in Suffolk and educated in Bury St Edmunds, was the first Governor of Massachusetts, and founded the city of Boston.

▲ *The 'Suffolk Trinity' at Rede Hall Farm Park.*

making are a legacy of the monks. It is said that the water was so unfit to drink in medieval times that the monks were allowed to consume up to eight pints of beer a day as their liquid intake. There were several brewhouses within the abbey precinct, and the Abbot had one all of his own to accommodate the thirsty requirements of his many visitors. As dawn breaks in Bury St Edmunds, you can smell the warm, wholesome aroma of malt wafting over the town from the Greene King brewery.

In the centre of town the Corn Exchange, an impressive Victorian building, is decorated with figures from agriculture, commerce and engineering. The weekly corn exchange took place here until very recently, but the site was formerly that of the Shambles or meat market. While the livestock market has also gone, a new farmers' market comes to town each month offering produce fresh from the local farms.

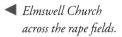
▲ *Pakenham Windmill.*

◀ *Elmswell Church across the rape fields.*

◀ *The Corn Exchange, now a venue for concerts, conferences, parties and fairs.*

13

MUCH-LOVED MARKET TOWN

Bury St Edmunds has long been at the heart of agriculture and commerce in west Suffolk. Its streets preserve in their names the trades of years gone by: Looms Lane, Buttermarket, Skinner Street and so on. They still retain the grid pattern devised by the abbots, making them easy to explore on foot. Fine façades reveal a wide range of unusual, independent shops offering traditional service and endless inspiration. In very few other towns can you buy a carpet-bag, a waistcoat and a didgeridoo all within the space of a few hundred yards. Shopping is a delight in Bury St Edmunds – and there are plenty of refreshment stops along the way.

The town has a strong tradition of markets and fairs, and the abbey benefited financially from all such occasions through fees and taxes. Angel Hill was probably designed for markets, and was the setting for the annual Bury Fair which took place for almost 600 years. This major social event was attended by traders, stallholders and entertainers from all over Europe. It was eventually discontinued in the 19th century on the grounds of immorality and nuisance to residents.

BURY FIRSTS
The first motor cycle side-car was designed and made by a Mr Montgomery in Brentgovel Street, Bury St Edmunds.

▶ *The twice-weekly provisions market in Buttermarket and Cornhill is a social event as well as a shopper's delight. Moyse's Hall is beyond.*

▲ *The Brewery Museum in Westgate Street, with an original mash tun outside.*

▲ *Market day in Bury St Edmunds.*

▼ *The Nutshell, the smallest pub in England. How many friends can you fit inside?*

The Art Gallery at Market Cross was built on the original stone cross that designated the official market place. Nowadays the twice-weekly provisions market flourishes in Butter-market and Cornhill. Almost 100 stalls sell everything from bonsai trees to the wares of London tailors, making it the largest weekly market in East Anglia.

A busy market town needs its shares of inns and alehouses, and Bury St Edmunds was indeed home to around 150 public houses in the 18th century. Whilst only a handful of these remain today, the town does boast the smallest pub in Britain, called The Nutshell. Brewers Greene King have been based in Bury St Edmunds for 200 years, and have named their Abbot Ale and St Edmund Ale in honour of the town's history. Remarkably, they draw water from the same wells that have been used for brewing since the 11th century.

15

FLORAL BURY ST EDMUNDS

Bury St Edmunds has been winning prizes for its floral displays over many years. The crowning glory is the Abbey Gardens, where 64 island beds set the standard for a mass of colour throughout the town each year in public planting, private gardens, office frontages, garage forecourts and school yards. These are the signs of the annual 'Bury in Bloom' campaign.

From children to centenarians, everyone plays a part in greening and cleaning the town. Such is their enthusiasm that Bury St Edmunds has enjoyed numerous wins in regional 'In Bloom' competitions. 1999 was the year when the town scooped the national Britain in Bloom prize for a second time, and brought home a 'Green Oscar' from the international Nations in Bloom competition.

A spring highlight for local people is the flowering of some 130,000 daffodils along an avenue of mature lime trees in Nowton Park. With its arboretum, wild flower meadows and wood sculptures, Nowton is the

BURY FIRSTS

Humphrey Repton (1752–1818), born in Bury St Edmunds, is considered by many to be the first great modern landscape architect, often referred to as the 'father of landscape gardening'.

perfect retreat from the bustle of town centre life. So too is its sister park, Hardwick Heath, with its tree gallery and 200-year-old cedars of Lebanon. The National Trust estate at Ickworth offers year-round interest, with an Italian garden, a sensory garden, a daffodil lawn, a 'Capability' Brown park and other beautiful horticultural features.

Between the Abbey Gardens and the cathedral lies the Pilgrims' Herb Garden. This is based on the Bury Herbal, a manuscript written in medieval times by the monks of the Abbey of St Edmund. Herb growers are plentiful in this part of Suffolk, and one well-known herbal author opens her garden to the public at Rougham.

Hanging baskets and planters deck the town centre throughout the summer.

◄ *A wood sculpture in Nowton Park.*

◄ *(inset) Floral beauty outside a Bury St Edmunds shop.*

▼ *Nowton Park in spring, with its daffodil avenue.*

AN INSPIRATION TO ARTISTS

It is not surprising that famous writers such as Charles Dickens and Daniel Defoe admired the charms of Bury St Edmunds. Indeed, William Cobbett called it 'the nicest town in the world'. Charles Dickens gave public readings at the Athenaeum, the town's assembly rooms on Angel Hill, and he stayed at the imposing Angel Hotel close by. The hotel features in his *Pickwick Papers* and visitors can still ask for the Charles Dickens suite and sleep in the author's bed. Novelist Norah Lofts lived in the splendid Northgate House and the prolific Victorian writer Ouida, born in Bury St Edmunds *c.*1840, is commemorated with a special statue just outside the town. Ouida was less enamoured of Bury St Edmunds, complaining that it was a dull town 'where people ring their own doorbells lest they grow rusty with disuse'. However the Chambers' Biographical Dictionary of 1897 did say her books displayed an 'encyclopaedic ignorance'.

▲ Moyse's Hall across the market, *a painting by Rose Mead.*

▼ *Street theatre at festival time.*

▼ *Bury St Edmunds Art Gallery.*

BURY FIRSTS
On 29 February 1892, the Theatre Royal, Bury St Edmunds, staged the first ever production of Charley's Aunt, the famous and enduring comedy by Brandon Thomas.

Artists have flourished in this area, with John Constable and Thomas Gainsborough taking their inspiration from the landscapes to the south-east of the town. Manor House Museum displays the work of three important female artists: Mary Beale, Rose Mead and Sybil Andrews, and there are exhibitions throughout the year in the cathedral cloisters. Look through the Norman tower for a statue of St Edmund by Suffolk artist Elisabeth Frink. Bury St Edmunds Art Gallery was designed by Robert Adam and is popular with lovers of art and architecture alike. The gallery runs a programme of nationally important displays and projects, together with a shop and a popular Christmas exhibition by the Suffolk Craft Society.

◄ *The intimate auditorium of the Theatre Royal.*

One of the best-loved buildings in the town is the Theatre Royal, one of the oldest working theatres of its size. Designed by William Wilkins, the architect of the National Gallery in London and Downing College Cambridge, it was opened in 1819 when the original theatre (now the Art Gallery) became too small for its audiences. At one stage, it closed and was used as a barrel store by Greene King brewery but was restored by the people of the town and granted on a 999 year lease to The National Trust. It is now a thriving venue for touring theatre, dance, music and comedy. It is a miniature of a West End theatre of great elegance, with a seating capacity of just 352, a tiny bar and a cosy foyer.

For a real explosion of artistic colour, nothing beats the Bury St Edmunds Festival in May. Starting with a military Beating Retreat ceremony on Angel Hill, the festival programme includes every kind of performing art from orchestral concerts to cookery, and from open-air jazz with fireworks to coffee-time talks. What more exciting way to explore the town's historic venues and open spaces?

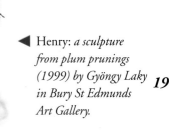

◄ Henry: *a sculpture from plum prunings (1999) by Gyöngy Laky in Bury St Edmunds Art Gallery.*

19

Good people all as you
Pas by, looke round
See how corpes do lye
For as you are sometime were we
And as we are so must you be.

Epitaph of Sarah Worton, 1698

Behind the fine architecture and floral excellence is a darker side to Bury St Edmunds. As the dusk gathers, a walk around the Great Churchyard (between the cathedral and St Mary's Church) reveals some fascinating tombstones commemorating the unfortunates of Bury St Edmunds. Hallowe'en walks with a ghostly Victorian graveyard warden are a perfect introduction to the Resurrection Men (better known as Bodysnatchers), to the local spectres and to the attempted murder of Edward Crispe by his mercenary brother-in-law Arundel Coke.

In the churchyard you will see the ruined Chapel of the Charnel, built before 1300 to house bones which had been dug up to make room for fresh burials. As the bones were stacked in the chapel vault, prayers were said by priests from the abbey. After the Dissolution the charnel house went on to become at various times a pub, a private house, and a blacksmith's shop. It carries the epitaphs of Sarah Lloyd and Mary Haselton, who met untimely deaths, the latter killed by lightning as she knelt to say her prayers.

◄ *The death mask of infamous 'Red Barn' murderer William Corder.*

Moyse's Hall (*c.*1180) is one of the oldest town houses in East Anglia. Over the years it has been a workhouse, a gaol, a police station and a railway parcels office but it now celebrates more than a century as the town's local history museum. Inside is a fine selection of unsavoury items such as man traps, gibbet cages and stone coffins. Mummified cats and wrinkled shoes, built into house walls to ward off evil spirits, show the superstitious side of Bury St Edmunds' past townsfolk. Most chilling of all, the relics of the Murder in the Red Barn, celebrated in Victorian melodrama, include the guilty William Corder's ear and a book bound in his skin!

BURY FIRSTS
Henry Crabbe-Robinson (1775–1867) who lived on Southgate Street, Bury St Edmunds, was the first foreign correspondent of *The Times*. He was a friend of both Wordsworth and Coleridge.